"I'm Not A Chef"
with Slices 'N Crumbs

Recipes and Shortcuts, Vol. 1
Appetizers, salads, entrees, snacks, and more!

A cookbook with
Slices 'N Crumbs owner

JUANITA S. GRAHAM

To order additional copies of this book, contact:
Xlibris
844-714-8691
www.Xlibris.com
Orders@Xlibris.com

Interior Image Credit: Juanita S. Graham

ISBN: Softcover   979-8-3694-2300-4
       Hardcover   979-8-3694-2301-1
       EBook   979-8-3694-2302-8

Library of Congress Control Number: 2024910489

Print information available on the last page

Rev. date: 08/20/2024

Contents

Introduction

Let's be clear, I am *not* a chef! Cooking is a form of art, and a "chef" is an artist. A chef's food is their masterpiece. I, on the other hand, am simply a young woman with a passion and desire to cook. There are people who have attended some of the most prestigious culinary schools, and have traveled the world to do so. From Italy to France, Spain to Africa, Beijing to Hawaii—they have studied just about everywhere! They have perfected a craft like no other. As for me, my studies began in my grandmother's kitchen—I did study travel and tourism, hospitality and hotel management in high school—but never pursued it further. Nevertheless, my ability to create flavorful, simple, and fun recipes for all ages is an honor. This cookbook was designed to make the "worse" cook feel comfortable in preparing delicious meals and dishes with step-by-step instructions and color illustrations. You will find that some recipes will have two variations: an intermediate version and an easy short-cut version. No matter which version you choose, you'll feel like a chef in the end! Well, maybe that's a bit extreme, but you'll definitely feel more confident about cooking. I will also provide you with ideas to assist with the food presentation.

Remember, there are two main components when it comes to cooking: presentation and taste. If the food looks good and/or appetizing, people will jump at the opportunity to have a taste. Parsley and paprika are by far the easiest "go-to" when it comes to presentation. Sprinkle a little here and a little there, and *boom*! You've officially taken the appearance up a few notches. Of course, there are more complex options to liven up your food presentation depending on the type of dish, such as edible flowers, arugula, sauces, etc. The next component, and most important, is obviously the taste. Many people make the mistake of rushing or trying to speed up the cooking process. This can often be the difference between delicious and disaster!

You can't prepare a full Thanksgiving dinner at 6:00 p.m. and you just started at 5:00 p.m. It just simply isn't going to happen. Unless you plan on ordering everything already prepared, of course. The point is that you have to give yourself adequate time to prep, cook, and serve. Nevertheless, although taste is the most important in my opinion, keep in mind that *everyone's* taste buds and palates are different. What may taste good to one may not be as desired to another. When cooking, we *all* cook according to our preferred taste of a particular dish. In most African American households and soul-food kitchens, it's said that you should season your dish until your ancestors tell you to stop. Jokingly, of course. Nevertheless, for some, this style may be too much seasoning. On the other hand, in most European households, it's thought that too much seasoning doesn't allow the food's natural flavors to flourish; while others may feel that salt and pepper are the only seasoning needed for any dish.

With this in mind, I always recommend seasoning food to your liking with a few exceptions. For example, take into consideration for whom you are preparing food. Ask yourself if they are elderly, diabetic, or if they are small children, then adjust accordingly (salt, sugar, spice, etc). All in all, cooking should be fun and not stressful. Simply think about what you want to cook or prepare and how you want it to look and don't rush the process! Thomas Edison said it best, "A vision without execution is hallucination." Now let's get started!

Pantry Tips

Many recipes call for items that we don't necessarily have *on hand*. Well, let's change that. Below is a list of a few basic items you should try to keep in your pantry at any given time. This may cut back on unnecessary grocery store runs right before dinner.

- Salt/pepper
- Granulated sugar
- Brown sugar
- Cinnamon
- Nutmeg
- All-purpose flour
- Thyme
- Sage
- Rosemary
- Oregano
- Parsley
- Extra virgin olive oil
- Paprika
- Basil
- Vanilla extract
- Garlic
- Italian seasoning or Herbs de Provence
- Slices 'N Crumbs everything spice

APPETIZERS

BRUSCHETTA

Prep time: 10 minutes
Cook time: 5–7 minutes
Makes 8–10 servings
Difficulty: 1 **2** 3 4 5

YOU WILL NEED:

1 French bread (baguette)
9 oz. tomatoes (cherry
   or grape, diced)
½ cup fresh basil (thinly sliced)
Parmesan cheese (grated)

2 garlic cloves (minced)
Bertolli balsamic glaze
Extra virgin olive oil
Sea salt (optional)
Ground black pepper (optional)

- Preheat oven to 450.
- Line a cookie sheet with parchment paper or foil.
- Place diced tomatoes in a large mixing bowl.
- Stir in basil, salt, pepper, and minced garlic; set mixture aside.
- Slice baguette diagonally into ½–¾ inch slices.
- Lightly brush each side with extra virgin olive oil.
- Place sliced baguettes on the cookie sheet and bake until golden brown and when they have a slight crunch. *Do* not *burn!*
- Remove from oven and transfer baguette to a serving tray or platter.
- Just before serving, top baguettes with tomato, basil, garlic, and salt mixture. *Note: Drain any juice from the mixture before topping the baguette. This will prevent the baguettes from becoming soggy.*
- Sprinkle with parmesan cheese.
- Drizzle with balsamic glaze.
- Serve immediately.

SHORTCUTS:

- Have the bakery slice the baguette for you or purchase a bundle of baguettes already sliced.
- Use prediced tomatoes.
- Use minced garlic in a jar (1 tsp equals approximately 2 cloves).

DEVILED EGGS

Prep time: 15 minutes
Cook time: 10 minutes
Makes 12 servings
Difficulty: 1 2 **3** 4 5

YOU WILL NEED:

6 large eggs
½ tbsp relish
½ tbsp mustard
¼ cup Miracle Whip salad dressing
¼ tsp salt

½ tsp sugar
¼ tsp pepper
Paprika (garnish)
Parsley (garnish)

- Boil eggs to a rolling boil for approximately 10 minutes.
- Remove from heat.
- Place boiled eggs in cold water to cool.
- Peel eggs and rinse.
- Slice eggs in half.
- Remove the center or egg yolks and place them in a mixing bowl.
- Place the outer egg on a serving platter or egg tray.
- Using a fork, smash the centers until there are very little lumps.
- Add relish, mustard, Miracle Whip, salt, sugar, and pepper
- Stir until well combined and somewhat smooth. *Do not overmix! Overmixing may cause the filling to be runny.*
- If additional Miracle Whip or mustard is desired, add 1 tsp at a time until the desired texture or consistency is accomplished.

- Fill a piping bag with egg mixture (if no piping bag is available, a spoon will work just as well).
- Fill each egg with equal amounts of mixture.
- Lightly sprinkle eggs with paprika and parsley to garnish.

DEVILED EGGS WITH SHRIMP

Prep time: 20 minutes
Cook time: 15 minutes
Makes 12 servings
Difficulty: 1 2 **3** 4 5

YOU WILL NEED:

6 large eggs
12 small to medium shrimps (tail on)
½ tbsp relish
½ tbsp mustard
¼ cup Miracle Whip salad dressing
¼ tsp salt

½ tsp sugar
¼ tsp pepper
Parsley (garnish)
1 tbsp butter
1 tbsp extra virgin olive oil
Old Bay or Cajun seasoning (to taste)

- Peel, devein, rinse, and pat shrimp dry. Do not remove the tail.
- Heat butter and extra virgin olive oil over medium to high heat.
- Add shrimp and season with Old Bay or cajun seasoning
- Cook for 2–3 minutes on each side. *Do* not *overcook!*
- Remove shrimp from the pan and set aside.
- Boil eggs to a rolling boil for approximately 10 minutes.
- Remove from heat and set aside.
- Place boiled eggs in cold water to cool.
- Peel eggs and rinse.
- Slice eggs in half
- Remove the center (egg yolks) and place in a mixing bowl.
- Place the outer egg on a serving platter or egg tray.
- Using a fork, smash the centers until there are very little lumps.
- Add relish, mustard, Miracle Whip, salt, sugar, and pepper.
- Stir until well combined and somewhat smooth. *Do* not *overmix! Overmixing may cause the filling to be runny.*
- If additional Miracle Whip or mustard is desired, add 1 tsp at a time until the desired texture or consistency is accomplished.
- Fill a piping bag with egg mixture. (If no piping bag is available, a spoon will work just as well.)
- Fill each egg with equal amounts of mixture.
- Place shrimp on top of each egg.
- Lightly sprinkle eggs with parsley to garnish.

- If you're short on time, simply use cocktail shrimp, sprinkle a little old bay on top, and garnish with parsley as usual.

FRIED RAVIOLI

Prep time: 15 minutes
Cook time: 10 minutes
Serves 1–2
Difficulty: **1** 2 3 4 5

YOU WILL NEED:

9 oz package of three-cheese
    ravioli (fresh, not frozen)
¼ cup milk
2 eggs
1–2 cups Italian breadcrumbs
1 cup vegetable oil

Grated parmesan cheese
Sea salt (optional)
Parsley (garnish)
Marinara sauce (for dipping)

- Heat oil over medium heat.
- In a large bowl, whisk eggs and milk until well combined.
- In a separate bowl, add breadcrumbs.
- Dip ravioli into the egg mixture, allowing the excess mixture to drip back into the bowl.
- Dip ravioli into breadcrumbs, covering completely.
- Fry a few ravioli at a time, making certain not to overcrowd the pan.
- Fry until golden brown for about 1–2 minutes per side. *Do* not *overcook!*
- Remove from pan and place on a paper towel to drain the excess oil.
- Transfer to a serving platter.
- Sprinkle with parmesan cheese or sea salt.
- Garnish with parsley.
- Serve with warmed marinara sauce for dipping.

Recipe for Love

Ingredients

A dash of Hope
1 cup of Affection
2 cups of Understanding
3 tbsp of Forgiveness

Take affection and mix thoroughly
with understanding before stirring in
hope and thoughtfulness. Blend together with
forgiveness. Bake with hugs and kisses.
Serve daily in generous portions.

8

LOADED CHICKEN NACHOS (*SHORTCUT)

Prep time: 10 minutes
Cook time: 10 minutes
Serves 2–4
Difficulty: 1 2 **3** 4 5

YOU WILL NEED:

1 17 oz bag of lime or guacamole
   flavor Tostitos tortilla chips
1 15 oz can of black beans
1 16 oz bag of Perdue
   chicken shortcuts
1 12 oz jar of jalapeno slices

1 8 oz container of sour cream
1 15 oz jar of Tostitos chunky salsa
1 8 oz pack of Mexican
   four-cheese blend
1 7 oz container of
   guacamole (optional)

- Preheat oven to 350.
- Cook black beans to a light simmer and set aside.
- Line an oven-safe dish with parchment paper.
- Arrange Tostitos tortilla chips in the dish. *It is not necessary to place them in a single layer!*
- Place chips in the oven for 3 minutes, just until warm. *Do* not *burn!*
- Remove from oven.
- Top the chips with black beans, the Perdue chicken shortcuts, and jalapeno slices
- Sprinkle with Mexican four-cheese blend
- Return chips to the oven and heat just until cheese melts.
- Remove from oven.
  - Top with a dollop of sour cream.

  - Serve with a side of guacamole and salsa.

SALADS

PASTA SALAD

Prep time: 15 minutes
Cook time: 20 minutes
Serves 4–6
Difficulty: 1 2 **3** 4 5

YOU WILL NEED:

1 12-16 oz box of tri-color pasta
1 2.25 oz can sliced black olives
1 cucumber (sliced and cut into fours)
1 red onion (sliced or diced)
2 ripe tomatoes (diced)
1 4.3 oz jar of McCormick
  Salad Supreme

16 oz of cheddar cheese crumbles
  or shredded cheddar cheese
1-2 16 oz bottles of Italian dressing
1 16 oz bag of Perdue chicken
  shortcuts (optional)

- Boil pasta as directed on the packaging. *Do* not *overcook!*
- Drain well.
- Rinse pasta with cold water to stop the cooking process and then drain again.
- Transfer to a large serving or mixing bowl and allow to cool completely.
- Wash/rinse cucumber, slice and cut each slice into fours, then set aside.
- Peel onion, then slice or dice (whichever is preferred) and set aside.
- Wash/rinse tomatoes, dice, and set aside.
- Drain olives and set aside.

- Once the pasta has cooled completely, add cucumber, onion, tomato, olives, chicken (optional), and cheese crumbles.
- Add Salad Supreme (to taste) and stir until well combined.
- Add 1 bottle of Italian dressing and stir until well combined.
- Refrigerate for 1–2 hours.
- Remove from refrigerator.
- Stir once again.
- Add additional Italian dressing if needed and stir before serving.

SHORTCUTS:

- Use 5 oz of prediced tomatoes and onions.

KALE SALAD

Prep time: 10 minutes
Serves 2–4
Difficulty: **1** 2 3 4 5

YOU WILL NEED:

1 bunch of kale or 1 bag of fresh
  kale (stems removed and
  cut into bite-size leaves)
¼ bag of shredded carrots
½ of 3.75 oz bag of Salad
  Pizzaz Strawberry Cranberry
  Honey Nut salad toppings

¼ cup of Ken's Steakhouse
  garlic and basil dressing
Grated parmesan cheese (optional)
1 lemon wedge for garnish

- Wash/rinse kale thoroughly and remove stems.
- Dry kale completely.
- In a large serving bowl, add kale, shredded carrots, salad toppings, and grated parmesan cheese.
- Toss until well combined.
- Gradually add the desired amount of Ken's Steakhouse garlic and basil dressing and toss until well coated.
- Garnish with lemon wedge.

TOMATO, CUCUMBER, ONION, AND MOZZARELLA SALAD

Prep time: 15 minutes
Serves 4–6
Difficulty: **1** 2 3 4 5

YOU WILL NEED:

12 oz of fresh whole tomato
  medley (cut in half)
1 package of mozzarella pearls
  (if mozzarella pearls are
  too large, cut in half)
½ tsp fresh thyme
½ tsp fresh rosemary
½ cup fresh basil (torn)

½ tbsp fresh parsley (for garnish)
½ English cucumber (cut into fours)
½ red onion (sliced)
3 tbsp extra virgin olive oil
1 tbsp of balsamic vinegar
Sea salt and cracked black
  pepper (to taste)

- In a large bowl, combine tomatoes, mozzarella pearls, thyme, rosemary, basil, cucumber, and red onion.
- In a separate bowl, whisk extra virgin olive oil, vinegar, salt, and pepper together until well combined.
- Drizzle dressing over the salad and toss.
- Cover with plastic wrap and refrigerate for approximately 30 minutes.
- Remove from refrigerator.
- Sprinkle the top with parsley for garnish.
- Serve immediately.

SALAMI, PEPPERONI, AND PROSCIUTTO SALAD

Prep time: 15 minutes
Serves 4–6
Difficulty: 1 **2** 3 4 5

YOU WILL NEED:

1 package of prosciutto
  (3–4 oz sliced)
1 package of Genoa
  salami (4 oz sliced)
1 package of Italian-style
  pepperoni (sliced)
1 English cucumber (cut into quarters)
½ red onion (sliced)
1 container of feta tomato and
  basil cheese crumbles

1 Avocado cut into bite-size chunks
1 pint of cherry tomatoes
2 Herbs de Provence or
  Italian seasoning
3 tbsp extra virgin olive oil
1 tbsp red wine vinegar
Salt and pepper (optional)

- Slice prosciutto, salami, and pepperoni and add to a large serving dish or bowl and set aside.
- Wash the cucumber and pat dry.
- Slice cucumber, cut slices into quarters, and add to the bowl.
- Slice red onion and add to the bowl.
- Remove the avocado from the outer skin, and remove the pit.
- Cut avocado into bite-size chunks and add to the bowl.
- Wash cherry tomatoes and pat dry.
- Cut cherry tomatoes in half and add to the bowl.

- Add feta cheese crumbles and Herbs de Provence or Italian seasoning to the bowl.
- In a separate bowl, whisk together extra virgin olive oil and red wine vinegar.
- Drizzle dressing over salad and combine well.
- Add salt and pepper to taste.

SEAFOOD SALAD

Prep time: 20 minutes
Cook time: 20–25 minutes
Serves 6–8
Difficulty: 1 2 **3** 4 5

YOU WILL NEED:

1 16 oz box of medium or large pasta shells
1 12 oz package of cooked, peeled, and deveined shrimp (if frozen, thaw completely)
1 8 oz container of lump crabmeat
1 8 oz package of imitation flake crab meat

1–2 celery stalks (diced)
1 small to medium onion (diced)
1 30 oz jar of Duke's mayonnaise
¼ cup of yellow mustard
Old Bay seasoning
Paprika (for garnish)

- Cook pasta shells according to packaging. Do *not* overcook!
- Remove from heat and drain completely.
- Rinse with cold water to stop the cooking process, then drain again.
- Transfer the pasta to a large serving bowl and allow to cool completely.
- Meanwhile, rinse shrimp and remove tails if necessary.
- Pat shrimp dry and set aside.
- In a separate bowl, empty crab meat, remove any shells, and set aside.
- Cut imitation crab meat into smaller, bite-size chunks.

- Dice celery and onion.
- Once pasta shells are completely cooled, add shrimp, crabmeat, imitation crab meat, celery, and onion.
- Season with Old Bay seasoning (to taste) and combine.
- Add an *entire* jar of Duke's mayonnaise.
- Add yellow mustard.
- Mix until well combined.
- Refrigerate for at least 2 hours.
- If additional Duke's mayonnaise is needed, add ¼ cup at a time until desired consistency and flavor is obtained.
- Just before serving, mix the pasta salad again.
- Sprinkle with paprika for garnish.

SHORTCUTS:

- Use prediced celery and onion.

SANDWICHES

PO BOY SANDWICH

Prep time: 20 minutes
Cook time: 15 minutes
Serves 2
Difficulty: 1 2 3 **4** 5

YOU WILL NEED:

2 blue catfish filets
1 lb large shrimp (peeled, deveined, tail removed)
1 bag Louisiana Fish Fry
1 bag Louisiana Shrimp Fry
2 tsp Old Bay or Cajun seasoning (divided)
⅛ cup of all-purpose flour
1 tsp paprika
1 tsp garlic powder

1 tsp onion powder
2 cups buttermilk
1 egg
Vegetable oil (for frying)
2 Italian or French sub rolls
Fresh romaine lettuce
1 ripe tomato (sliced)
Remoulade sauce
Pickle spears

PREPARING THE FISH:

- Heat oil to 350 degrees.
- Rinse fish and pat dry.

- In a large bowl, add Louisiana Fish Fry, all-purpose flour, 1 tsp of Old Bay or Cajun seasoning, paprika, garlic powder, and onion powder.
- Mix until well combined.
- In a separate bowl, combine buttermilk and egg.
- Whisk until well combined.
- Submerge fish in buttermilk and egg mixture, coating completely.
- Remove fish from the mixture, allowing the excess mixture to drip back into the bowl.
- Toss fish in Louisiana Fish Fry mixture.
- Shake off any extra mixture.
- Fry fish until golden brown and is cooked throughout.
- Remove from oil and place on a paper towel to drain remaining oil.

PREPARING THE SHRIMP

- Heat oil to 350 degrees.
- Rinse and pat dry.
- In a large bowl, add Louisiana Shrimp Fry and 1 tsp of Old Bay or Cajun seasoning.
- Mix until well combined.
- Toss shrimp in Louisiana Shrimp Fry mixture.
- Shake off any extra mixture.
- Fry shrimp until golden brown. *Do* not *overcook!*
- Remove from oil and place on a paper towel to drain remaining oil.

PREPARING THE SANDWICH

- Rinse lettuce and dry completely.
- Lightly toast sub rolls (optional).
- Spread the desired amount of remoulade on sub rolls.
- Add the desired amount of lettuce and tomato slices to each sub roll.
- Add catfish filet to each sub roll.
- Add the desired amount of shrimp to each sub roll.

- Cut each Po Boy sandwich in half (optional).
- Garnish with pickle spear.

CLASSIC BLT WITH AVOCADO

Prep time: 10 minutes
Cook time: 10 minutes
Serves 1
Difficulty: **1** 2 3 4 5

YOU WILL NEED:

3 strips of thick-cut bacon
1 ripe tomato (sliced)
1 avocado (sliced)
Romaine lettuce

Duke's mayonnaise
2 slices of rye bread
Salt and pepper (optional)

- Fry bacon until fully cooked. *Do not overcook or burn!*
- Rinse lettuce, dry completely, and set aside.
- Remove bacon from the pan and drain on a paper towel.
- Toast bread to desired darkness.
- Transfer to a serving plate.
- Spread the desired amount of Duke's mayonnaise on both slices of bread.
- Assemble one slice of bread with lettuce, tomato slices, avocado slices, and bacon.
- Lightly sprinkle with salt and pepper (optional).
- Top with a second slice of bread.
- Cut the sandwich in half and serve.

GRINDER SANDWICH

Prep time: 10 minutes
Cook time: 5 minutes
Serves 2
Difficulty: 1 2 **3** 4 5

YOU WILL NEED:

2 Italian sub rolls
1 8 oz bag of iceberg
   lettuce (shredded)
1 red onion (sliced)
½ of a 12 oz jar of Mt. Olive Sweet
   Salad Banana Peppers (drained)
½ cup of Duke's mayonnaise
Dijon mustard
2 ½ tbsp of red wine vinegar
1 tbsp of Herbs de Provence
   or Italian seasoning

Kosher salt and cracked black
   pepper (to taste)
Swiss or provolone cheese
Deli turkey
Deli ham
Genoa salami
Prosciutto
2 tomatoes (sliced)
Parmesan cheese (finely grated)

- Preheat oven to 350.
- In a large mixing bowl, combine shredded lettuce, sliced red onion, sweet salad peppers, mayonnaise, red wine vinegar, Herbs de Provence or Italian seasoning, parmesan cheese, and salt and pepper.
- Mix until well combined and set aside.

- Place sub rolls on a baking sheet.
- Add the desired amount of turkey, ham, salami, prosciutto, and cheese to one side of the sub rolls.
- Heat until cheese is melted, about 3–4 minutes.
- Remove from oven.
- Add the desired amount of grinder mixture to each sub roll.
- Top each sub roll with tomato slices.
- Drizzle with Dijon mustard.
- Cut sandwiches in half and serve with pickle spears and chips.

SOFT SHELL CRAB

Prep time: 13 minutes
Cook time: 6-8 minutes
Serves 2
Difficulty: 1 2 **3** 4 5

YOU WILL NEED:

2 soft shell crabs (cleaned)
2 Kaiser rolls or buns
1 large egg
1 cup milk
1 tsp hot sauce
Romaine lettuce

1 tomato (sliced)
1 cup all-purpose flour
½ tbsp of Old Bay seasoning
Remoulade
Pickles
Vegetable oil

- Preheat oil to 350.
- Combine flour and Old Bay seasoning.
- In a separate bowl, whisk together milk, hot sauce, and egg.
- Dredge *cleaned* soft shell crabs in the milk mixture and ensure the crabs are covered completely.
- Remove from milk mixture, and coat each soft shell crab in flour mixture.
- Shake off excess flour.
- Fry soft shell crabs until golden brown (approximately 6 minutes, turning midway through frying).

- Remove from oil and drain on a paper towel.
- On the bottom portion of the Kaiser roll, place desired amount of lettuce, sliced tomatoes, and pickles.
- Add soft-shell crab.
- On the top bun, spread the desired amount of remoulade sauce.
- Serve with chips or fries.

PASTA

HOMEMADE MACARONI AND CHEESE

Prep time: 20 minutes
Cook time: 40 minutes
Serves 6–8
Difficulty: 1 2 3 **4** 5

YOU WILL NEED:

1 box of elbow macaroni
1 can of evaporated milk
1 cup of whole milk
16 oz of extra sharp cheddar
  cheese (shredded and divided)
16 oz of mild cheddar cheese
  (shredded and divided)

16 oz of Colby Jack cheese
  (shredded and divided)
1 large egg
2 tbsp of butter
1 tbsp of paprika
2 tbsp of yellow mustard
Salt and cracked pepper to taste
Parsley for garnish

- Preheat oven to 375.
- Boil macaroni just until *al dente. Do* not *overcook!*
- Remove macaroni from heat and drain.
- Transfer macaroni to large mixing bowl.
- Add evaporated milk, whole milk, half of the extra sharp cheddar, mild cheddar, and colby jack, egg, butter, paprika, mustard, salt and pepper.
- Stir until well combined (add more milk ¼ cup at a time if necessary).
- Lightly grease a casserole dish with butter.

- Pour macaroni into casserole dish.
- Cover with foil and bake for 30–35 minutes
- While the macaroni is baking, mix the remaining cheeses together.
- Remove macaroni from oven and remove foil.
- Top with remaining cheese.
- Return macaroni to oven and bake uncovered until cheese melted and sides have a slight crisp, approximately 10–13 minutes.
- Remove from oven and garnish with parsley.
- Allow to cool somewhat before cutting.

HOMEMADE SEAFOOD MACARONI AND CHEESE

Prep time: 25 minutes
Cook time: 40 minutes
Serves 6–8
Difficulty: 1 2 3 **4** 5

YOU WILL NEED:

½ lb of large shrimp (cooked and tail removed)
3 small to medium lobster tails (cooked and cut into bite-size pieces)
1 box of Cavatappi noodles
1 can of evaporated milk
1 ½ cups of whole milk
6 oz of Fontina cheese
6 oz of Gouda cheese
6 oz of Gruyere cheese
16 oz of extra sharp cheddar cheese (shredded and divided)

16 oz of mild cheddar cheese (shredded and divided)
24 oz of Colby Jack cheese (shredded and divided)
1–2 large eggs
1–2 tbsp of butter
½ tsp of paprika
1 tbsp Old Bay seasoning
¼ cup of Panko breadcrumbs
2 tbsp of yellow mustard
Salt and cracked pepper to taste
Parsley for garnish

- Preheat oven to 375.
- Boil macaroni just until *al dente. Do* not *overcook!*
- Remove noodles from heat and drain.
- Transfer noodles to a large mixing bowl.
- Add evaporated milk, whole milk, fontina cheese, gouda cheese, half of the extra sharp cheddar, mild cheddar, and Colby Jack cheeses, egg, butter, paprika, old bay, mustard, salt, and pepper.
- Stir until well combined (add more milk ⅛ cup at a time if necessary).
- Lightly grease a casserole dish with butter.
- Pour ½ of the mixture into the casserole dish.
- Add ½ of the shrimp and lobster.
- Add another ¼ of the mixture to the casserole dish.
- Add remaining shrimp and lobster.

- Add the remaining noodle mixture to the casserole dish.
- Cover with foil and bake for 35–40 minutes
- While the noodles are baking, mix the remaining cheeses together.
- Remove the casserole dish from the oven and remove the foil.
- Top with remaining cheese and breadcrumbs.
- Return dish to oven and bake uncovered until cheese melted, and sides have a slight crisp, approximately 10–13 minutes.
- Remove from oven and garnish with parsley.
- Allow to cool somewhat before cutting.

MEAT LASAGNA (*SHORTCUTS)

Prep time: 10 minutes
Cook time: 35 minutes
Serves 4–6
Difficulty: 1 2 **3** 4 5

YOU WILL NEED:

1 box of San Giorgio
    oven-ready lasagna
24 oz Ragu Chunky Garden
    Combination pasta sauce
24 oz Ragu Chunky Mushroom
    and Green Pepper pasta sauce
1–2 lb ground hamburger
1 tbsp oregano
1 tsp sage

1 tsp thyme
1 tsp rosemary
¼ tsp onion powder
¼ tsp garlic powder
¼ tsp salt and pepper
1 tbsp McCormick's
    hamburger seasoning
32 oz mozzarella cheese (shredded)
Parsley for garnish

- Preheat oven to 350.
- Cook ground hamburger until there are no traces of pink.
- Season with McCormick's hamburger seasoning.
- Remove from heat and drain well.
- Over medium-high heat, heat pasta sauce to a simmer.
- Add oregano, thyme, sage, rosemary, onion powder, garlic, salt, and pepper.
- Stir well.
- Add hamburger, stir well.
- Remove from heat.
- In a casserole dish, add oven-ready lasagna in a single layer.
- Using a ladle, spoon sauce on top of lasagna until covered.
- Sprinkle with mozzarella cheese until covered.
- Repeat steps (lasagna, sauce, mozzarella) 2–3 more times.
- Be sure not to overfill the casserole dish.
- Bake uncovered for 30 minutes.
- Remove from heat.
- Garnish with parsley.
- Allow to cool slightly before cutting.
- Serve with garlic bread and Caesar's salad.

STUFFED PASTA SHELLS

Prep time: 20 minutes
Cook time: 30 minutes
Serves 4–6
Difficulty: 1 2 **3** 4 5

YOU WILL NEED:

1 box of San Giorgio
   jumbo pasta shells
16 oz Bertolli olive oil and
   garlic pasta sauce
1 large egg
1 tbsp oregano
1 tbsp thyme
1 tbsp rosemary

Salt and cracked black
   pepper (to taste)
16 oz mozzarella cheese
   (shredded and divided)
32 oz ricotta cheese
7 oz parmesan cheese
Parsley for garnish

- Preheat oven to 350.
- Cook pasta shells according to packaging. *Do* not *overcook!*
- Remove from heat and drain well.
- In a large mixing bowl, combine ricotta cheese, egg, oregano, thyme, rosemary, parmesan cheese, and half of mozzarella cheese.
- Combine well.
- Using a spoon, stuff shells with mixture.
- In a casserole dish, spread a small amount of pasta sauce in a thin layer, covering the bottom of the dish.
- Add stuffed shells.
- Sprinkle with remaining mozzarella cheese.
- Bake uncovered for 25–30 minutes.
- Remove from heat.
- Garnish with parsley.

POT PIES AND QUICHE

CLASSIC CHICKEN POT PIE (*SHORTCUTS)

Prep time: 20 minutes
Cook time: 35-45 minutes
Serves 2–4
Difficulty: 1 2 3 **4** 5

YOU WILL NEED:

1 bag of Perdue chicken shortcuts
(cut into bite-size pieces)
1 bag of Country Blend vegetables
or mixed vegetables
3-4 small red potatoes (cut
into bite-size pieces)
1 can of cream of celery

¼ cup of heavy cream
½ cup of milk
1 egg
1 tsp of water
Salt and pepper (to taste)
2 deep-dish pie shells

- Preheat oven to 375.
- Boil potatoes. *Do* not *overcook!*
- Cook vegetables according to packaging.
- Separate pie shells and set aside.
- Mix egg and water together and then set aside.
- Remove potatoes from the heat, then drain.
- Drain vegetables and add them to the pot of potatoes.
- Add cream of celery, heavy cream, milk, chicken, and salt and pepper to pot.
- Stir until combined.
- Return to heat and let cook for 3 minutes.
- Pour mixture into one pie shell. *Do* not *overfill!*
- Carefully flip the second pie shell upside down on top of the first pie shell.
- Carefully remove the outer aluminum pan.
- Use a fork to seal the edges by pressing firmly.
- Brush pie and edges with egg wash.
- Bake for 35–45 minutes until golden brown.
- Remove from oven.
- Allow to cool slightly before serving because filling will be extremely hot.

SHORTCUTS:

- Mini red potatoes may be used as well. Be sure to cut them in half, if necessary.

BUFFALO CHICKEN POT PIE

Prep time: 20 minutes
Cook time: 35–45 minutes
Serves 2–4
Difficulty: 1 2 3 **4** 5

YOU WILL NEED:

1 bag of Perdue chicken shortcuts
   (cut into bite-size pieces)
1 bag of Country Blend vegetables
   or mixed vegetables
3–4 small red potatoes (cut
   into bite-size pieces)
1 can of cream of celery
½ cup of heavy cream

½ cup of milk
⅛ cup buffalo sauce
¼ cup of bleu cheese crumbles
1 egg
1 tsp of water
Salt and pepper (to taste)
2 deep-dish pie shells

- Preheat oven to 375.
- Boil potatoes. *Do* not *overcook!*
- Cook vegetables according to packaging.
- Separate pie shells and set aside.
- Mix egg and water together and then set aside.
- Remove potatoes from heat and then drain.
- Drain vegetables and add them to the pot of potatoes.
- Add cream of celery, heavy cream, milk, buffalo sauce, bleu cheese crumbles, chicken, and salt and pepper to the pot.
- Stir until well combined.
- Return to heat and let cook for 3 minutes.
- Pour mixture into one pie shell. *Do* not *overfill!*
- Carefully flip the second pie shell upside down, on top of the first pie shell.
- Carefully remove the outer aluminum pan.
- Use a fork to seal the edges by pressing firmly.
- Brush pie and edges with egg wash.
- Bake for 35–45 minutes until golden brown.
- Remove from oven.
- Allow to cool slightly before serving as filling will be extremely hot.

SHORTCUTS:

- Mini red potatoes may be used as well. Be sure to cut them in half, if necessary.

SEAFOOD POT PIE

Prep time: 20 minutes
Cook time: 35–45 minutes
Serves 4–6
Makes 2 pies
Difficulty: 1 2 3 **4** 5

YOU WILL NEED:

1 bag of Country Blend vegetables or mixed vegetables
3–4 small red potatoes (cut into bite-size pieces)
1–2 cans of cream of celery
½ cup of heavy cream
1 cup of milk
½ pound of large shrimp (cleaned, deveined, tail removed)

2 small lobster tails (steamed and cut into bite-size pieces)
6 sea scallops (cleaned and membrane removed)
8 oz jumbo lump crabmeat (shells removed)
2 egg
2 tsp of water
Old Bay seasoning (to taste)
4 deep-dish pie shells

- Preheat oven to 375.
- Boil potatoes. *Do* not *overcook!*
- Cook vegetables according to packaging instructions.
- Separate pie shells and then set aside.
- Mix egg and water together and then set aside,
- Remove potatoes from heat then drain.
- Drain vegetables and add them to the pot of potatoes.
- Add cream of celery, heavy cream, milk, shrimp, scallops, lobster, crabmeat, and Old Bay to the pot.

- Stir until well combined.
- Return to heat and let cook for 3 minutes.
- Pour mixture into two pie shells. *Do* not *overfill!*
- Carefully flip the second pie shells upside down, placing one shell each, on top of the first pie shells.
- Carefully remove the outer aluminum pans.
- Use a fork to seal the edges of each pie by pressing firmly.
- Brush each pie and edges with egg wash.
- Bake for 35–45 minutes until golden brown.
- Remove from oven.
- Allow to cool slightly before serving as the filling will be extremely hot.

- Mini red potatoes may be used as well. Be sure to cut them in half, if necessary.

VEGETABLE POT PIE

Prep time: 20 minutes
Cook time: 35–45 minutes
Serves 2–4
Difficulty: 1 2 **3** 4 5

YOU WILL NEED:

1 bag of Country Blend vegetables
    or mixed vegetables
3–4 small red potatoes (cut
    into bite-size pieces)
1 can of cream of celery
½ cup of heavy cream

½ cup of milk
1 egg
1 tsp of water
Salt and pepper (to taste)
2 deep-dish pie shells

- Preheat oven to 375.
- Boil potatoes. *Do* not *overcook!*
- Cook vegetables according to packaging instructions.
- Separate pie shells and then set aside.
- Mix egg and water together and then set aside.
- Remove potatoes from heat and then drain.
- Drain vegetables and add them to the pot of potatoes.
- Add cream of celery, heavy cream, milk, and salt and pepper to the pot.
- Stir until well combined.
- Return to heat and let cook for 3 minutes.
- Pour mixture into one pie shell. *Do* not *overfill!*

- Carefully flip the second pie shell upside down, on top of the first pie shell.
- Carefully remove the outer aluminum pan.
- Use a fork to seal the edges by pressing firmly.
- Brush pie and edges with egg wash.
- Bake 35–45 minutes until golden brown.
- Remove from the oven.
- Allow to cool slightly before serving as the filling will be extremely hot.

SHORTCUTS:

- Mini red potatoes may be used as well. Be sure to cut them in half, if necessary.

SPINACH AND CARROT QUICHE

Prep time: 15 minutes
Cook time: 50–60 minutes
Serves 6-8
Difficulty: 1 2 **3** 4 5

YOU WILL NEED:

2 pie shells (thawed/refrigerated)
1 package of frozen spinach
   (thawed and drained well)
1 ½ cup of shredded carrots
1 tbsp of dried marjoram
1 tbsp of Herbs de Provence
2 cups of milk or heavy cream

4 eggs
½ cup of Gruyere cheese
½ cup of Muenster cheese
½ cup of Feta tomato and
   basil cheese crumbles
½ tsp of lemon juice
Salt and pepper to taste

- Preheat oven to 350.
- In a bowl, whisk together eggs, lemon juice, and milk or heavy cream.
- In a separate bowl, combine spinach, carrots, cheeses, and seasonings.
- Using a fork, pierce the bottom of each pie shell sporadically a few times.
- Bake pie shells approximately for 4–5 minutes.
- Remove pie shells from the oven and fill each pie shell evenly with spinach, carrot, and cheese mixture.
- Pour egg mixture evenly over spinach, carrot, and cheese mixture.

- Return pies to oven and bake for 50–60 minutes until quiche is cooked throughout and firm.
- Remove from oven.
- Allow to cool slightly before serving.

BROCCOLI AND CHEESE CASSEROLE

Prep time: 15 minutes
Cook time: 25–30 minutes
Serves 4–6
Difficulty: 1 **2** 3 4 5

YOU WILL NEED:

12 oz frozen broccoli
1 ½ cups of shredded
   Colby Jack cheese
1 can of cream of mushroom
   or cream of celery coup
½ cup of milk or heavy cream

½ tsp garlic powder
½ tsp pepper
1 tbsp Mrs. Dash original seasoning
1 ½ tbsp butter (melted)
½ cup of panko breadcrumbs

- Preheat oven to 350.
- Steam broccoli for approximately 2–3 minutes.
- Remove broccoli and place in ice water to stop the cooking process.
- In a separate bowl, combine soup, milk, a cup of cheese, and seasonings.
- Drain broccoli completely.
- Add broccoli to soup, milk, and cheese mixture.
- Stir until well combined.
- Pour mixture into casserole dish.
- Mix melted butter and panko breadcrumbs together.
- Sprinkle the remaining cheese on top of the casserole.
- Add breadcrumbs on top.
- Bake uncovered for approximately for 25–30 minutes or until golden brown and cheese is melted.

- Remove from the oven and allow to cool slightly before serving. The cheese will be extremely hot.

BEEF, CHICKEN, AND PORK

LAMB CHOPS

Prep time: 10 minutes
Cook time: 5–6 minutes
Serves 2–4
Difficulty: 1 **2** 3 4 5

YOU WILL NEED:

1 rack of lamb cut into chops
  (1 rack usually makes
  approximately 8 chops)
Extra virgin olive oil
1 tsp of dried thyme
1 tsp of rosemary
1 tsp of dried marjoram

½ tsp of minced garlic
½ tsp of cumin
½ tsp Worcestershire sauce
1 tsp of mustard
Salt and pepper to taste
Parsley (optional)

- Clean lamb chops and pat dry.
- In a large mixing bowl, add lamb chops and all ingredients.
- Gently massage ingredients onto the lamb chop and ensure that they are coated evenly; set aside.
- Lightly coat a skillet with extra virgin olive oil and heat for a few seconds on medium heat. *Do not burn the oil! A few seconds is all you need as olive oil burns fast!*
- Add a few lamb chops to the skillet, being sure not to overcrowd the skillet.
- Cook over medium to high heat, about 3–4 minutes per side.

- Remove lamb chops from skillet.
- Transfer to a serving tray and garnish with parsley.

OVEN-BAKED PORK RIBS

Prep time: 10 minutes
Cook time: 3 hours
Serves 2–4
Difficulty: 1 **2** 3 4 5

YOU WILL NEED:

1 slab of baby back ribs
1 tbsp Mc Cormick's Grill Mates
   Smokehouse maple seasoning
¼ cup of brown sugar
½ tbsp cumin
½ tsp onion powder

½ tbsp garlic powder
½ mustard powder
½ smoked paprika
¼ tbsp cayenne pepper
18 oz of Sticky Fingers Carolina
   sweet bar-b-que sauce

- Preheat oven to 325.
- Clean ribs and pat dry.
- Combine all ingredients in a bowl until well incorporated.
- Generously massage both sides of the ribs with seasoning.
- Line an oven tray with aluminum foil.
- Transfer the ribs to the tray and place them in the oven.
- Bake for 45 minutes.
- After 45 minutes, turn the ribs on the other side and bake for an additional 45 minutes.
- After 45 minutes, turn the ribs over again, coat them with bar-b-que sauce, and bake for 30 minutes.

- After 30 minutes, turn the ribs over, coat them with bar-b-que sauce, and bake for an additional 30 minutes.
- After 30 minutes, turn the ribs over, coat them with bar-b-que sauce, and bake for 15 minutes.
- After 15 minutes, turn the ribs over, coat them with bar-b-que sauce, and bake for 5 minutes.
- After 5 minutes, turn the ribs over, coat them with bar-b-que sauce one last time, and bake for 5 minutes.
- Remove from the oven.
- Transfer to a serving tray and enjoy.

BAKED CHICKEN AND PEPPERS

Prep time: 10 minutes
Cook time: 1 hour–1 hour 15 minutes
Serves 3–5
Difficulty: 1 **2** 3 4 5

YOU WILL NEED:

6 chicken thighs
1 cup of chicken broth
1 red pepper (sliced)
1 green pepper (sliced)
1 yellow pepper (sliced)
½ onion (sliced)

1 tbsp smoked paprika
1 ½ tbsp garlic powder
1 ½ tbsp Herbs de Provence
2 tbsp Mc Cormick's Grill Mates
   Montreal chicken seasoning

- Preheat oven to 375.
- Clean chicken and pat dry.
- Combine smoked paprika, garlic powder, Herbs de Provence, and Mc Cormick's.
- Place chicken in a large bowl and add seasoning blend.
- Massage seasoning on chicken, coating completely.
- Add chicken broth to a baking dish.
- Transfer chicken to a baking dish.
- Add peppers and onion.
- Cover with aluminum foil.

- Using a fork or knife, make a few hole on top of the aluminum foil.
- Bake for 30 minutes.
- After 30 minutes, remove the foil and baste the chicken.
- Return chicken to the oven, and bake uncovered for 30–35 minutes, basting every 10 minutes.
- Remove chicken from oven and transfer to a serving plate.
- Garnish with parsley.

NOTE:

- For extra crispy skin, place the chicken under the broiler for 2–4 minutes.
- Remove from broiler and baste.

BEEF LIVER AND ONIONS

Prep time: 5 minutes
Cook time: 5–7 minutes
Serves 2
Difficulty: 1 **2** 3 4 5

2 beef livers	Extra virgin olive oil
½ small onion (sliced)	5 oz of Gravy Master
½-¾ cup of all-purpose flour	Salt and pepper to taste
4 tbsp of butter	

- Lightly coat skillet with extra virgin olive oil and 1 tbsp of butter.
- Warm skillet over medium heat.
- Coat both sides of the liver in flour.
- Add liver to skillet and fry for 2–3 minutes per side.
- Remove livers from the pan and set aside.
- Add 1 tbsp of butter and onions to skillet.
- Saute until onions are soft.
- Remove onions and set aside.
- Add 2 tbsp of butter to the skillet.
- Gradually add flour (1 tbsp at a time) and stir continuously.
- Gradually add Gravy Master and continue to stir until smooth.
- Add salt and pepper, if desired.
- Simmer for 3 minutes.
- Return liver and onions to skillet with gravy.
- Cover and simmer for 3–5 minutes.
- Remove skillet from heat.
- Plate and serve.

SWEET AND SAVORY MEATBALLS

Prep time: 15 minutes
Cook time: 60 minutes
Serves 6–8
Difficulty: 1 2 **3** 4 5

YOU WILL NEED:

1-2 bags of homestyle meatballs
⅔ cup of orange marmalade
32 oz of grape jelly
¼ cup of Thai-style sweet chili sauce

18 oz of Stubbs Hickory Bourbon
   bar-b-que sauce ½
½ lemon (juice only)
½ can of pineapple chunks (drained)
Salt and pepper to taste

- Preheat oven to 375.
- In a medium pot, over medium-to-high heat, whisk together orange marmalade, grape jelly, and Thai sweet chili sauce until smooth consistency is achieved.
- Squeeze in the juice of ½ lemon and whisk together.
- Add bar-b-que sauce and whisk.
- Simmer for 3–5 minutes, stirring frequently.
- Remove from heat.
- Add meatballs to a casserole dish or aluminum pan.
- Spread pineapple chunks on top.
- Pour sauce over meatballs.
- Bake covered for 40–45 minutes.
- Remove the cover and stir.

- Return to oven and bake for an additional 15–20 minutes without cover.
- Remove from the oven and stir again before serving.
- Caution: *The sauce will be hot!*

CROCKPOT CHUCK ROAST

Prep time: 10 minutes
Cook time: 5 hours
Serves 4–6
Difficulty: 1 2 **3** 4 5

YOU WILL NEED:

2-3 lb chuck roast
2-2 ½ cups of beef broth
2 oz of red wine (optional)
2 tbsp McCormick Grill Mates
   hamburger seasoning
2 tbsp McCormick Grill Mates
   Brazilian steakhouse seasoning

2 garlic cloves
Salt (to taste)
Pepper (to taste)
1 tbsp butter
1 tbsp extra virgin olive oil

- Heat oil and butter in a skillet over medium-to-high heat.
- Season both sides of chuck roast with McCormick seasonings, salt, and pepper.
- Once the skillet is heated, transfer the roast to the skillet.
- Sear roast on both sides for about 3 minutes.
- Pour beef broth and red wine into crock pot.
- Add garlic cloves.
- Add chuck roast to crock pot.
- Cover and cook on high heat for 4 to 4.5 hours or until desired tenderness is achieved.
- Once roast has cooked, remove from crockpot and transfer to a serving dish.
- Allow roast to rest approximately 10 minutes before cutting.

SALSA AND SALAD DRESSINGS

MANGO SALSA (*SHORTCUTS)

Prep time: 10 minutes
Cook time: 10 minutes
Serves 2
Difficulty: **1** 2 3 4 5

YOU WILL NEED:

15 oz of Del Monte diced
    mangos (drained)
2.5 oz of diced tomatoes
½ red onion (diced)
.35 oz of Gourmet Garden cilantro

1 jalapeno pepper (seeded and diced)
1 lime (juice only)
½ tbsp of minced garlic
Salt and pepper to taste

- In a large mixing bowl, combine all ingredients.
- Cover and refrigerate for 10–15 minutes.
- Remove from refrigerator and transfer to a serving bowl.
- Serve with tortilla chips or fish tacos.

PICO DE GALLO

Prep time: 10 minutes
Cook time: 5 minutes
Serves 2–4
Difficulty: 1 **2** 3 4 5

YOU WILL NEED:

5.0 oz of tomatoes (diced)
5.0 oz of onion (diced)
.35 oz of Gourmet Garden cilantro
1-2 jalapeno pepper
   (seeded and diced)

1 lime (juice only)
1 tbsp of minced garlic
Salt to taste

- In a large mixing bowl, combine all ingredients until well incorporated.
- Cover and refrigerate for 10–15 minutes.
- Remove from refrigerator and transfer to a serving bowl.
- Serve with tortilla chips or fish tacos.

SHORTCUTS:

- Use prediced tomatoes and onions.

GUACAMOLE

Prep time: 10 minutes
Cook time: 10 minutes
Serves 1
Difficulty: 1 **2** 3 4 5

YOU WILL NEED:

1 avocado
1 tbsp of diced red onion
2 tbsp of diced tomato
1 jalapeno pepper (chopped and seeded)

1 ½ tbsp cilantro (finely chopped)
½ tbsp of minced garlic
¼ tsp sea salt
½ lime (juice)

- Cut avocado in half and remove seed.
- Scoop avocado into a small bowl.
- Using a fork, smash avocado into small chunks.
- Add remaining ingredients to bowl with avocado
- Stir until well combined.
- Serve with chips and salsa.

PINEAPPLE AND MANGO SALSA

Prep time:
Cook time:
Serves
Difficulty: 1 2 **3** 4 5

YOU WILL NEED:

15 oz of Del Monte diced
    mangos (drained)
15.25 oz of Del Monte
    pineapple tidbits
5 oz of diced tomatoes
½ red onion (diced)

.35 oz of Gourmet Garden cilantro
2 jalapeno pepper (seeded and diced)
1 lime (juice only)
1 tbsp of minced garlic
Salt and pepper to taste

- In a large mixing bowl, combine all ingredients.
- Cover and refrigerate for 10–15 minutes.
- Remove from refrigerator and transfer to a serving bowl.
- Serve with tortilla chips or fish tacos.

HOMEMADE SALAD DRESSING

Prep time: 10 minutes
Cook time: 5 minutes
Serves 2–4
Difficulty: **1** 2 3 4 5

YOU WILL NEED:

8.5 oz of extra virgin olive oil
2 tbsp of dried thyme
2 tbsp of dried rosemary
2 tbsp of dried marjoram
2 tbsp of dried basil

½ tbsp of minced garlic
¼ tsp of salt
¼ tsp of pepper
1 tbsp of red wine vinegar

- Whisk together all ingredients until well combined.
- Drizzle over salad.

Note: Pour dressing into a saucer, add ½ tsp of crushed red pepper flakes, and dip your favorite bread.

DESSERTS

BANANA PUDDING

Prep time: 5 minutes
Cook time: 10 minutes
Serves 4–6
Difficulty: 1 2 **3** 4 5

YOU WILL NEED:

1 5.1 oz box of banana cream
    instant pudding
3 cups of milk (cold)
8 oz of Philadelphia cream
    cheese (softened)
8 oz Cool Whip (room temperature)

14 oz sweet condensed milk
1–2 large bananas
1 box of vanilla wafers or
    Chessman cookies
¼ tsp of banana extract

- In a large mixing bowl, combine banana cream instant pudding and milk.
- Whisk together for about 2–3 minutes and then set aside.
- In a separate mixing bowl, combine cream cheese, condensed milk, and banana extract.
- Mix until there are very little lumps.
- Fold whipped cream into the mixture until completely combined.
- Fold banana pudding into mixture until well combined and then set aside.
- In a casserole dish, add a single layer of vanilla wafers.
- Slice 1 banana on top of wafers.
- Pour about half of the banana pudding on top of the sliced banana and wafers.
- Repeat the last three steps until the casserole dish is filled.
- Sporadically layer vanilla wafers on the top (this should be the final layer).
- Crumble 10–15 wafers and sprinkle on top.
- Cover and refrigerate for 2–3 hours before serving.

Recipe for Love

Ingredients

A dash of Hope
1 cup of Affection
2 cups of Understanding
3 tbsp of Forgiveness

Take affection and mix thoroughly
with understanding before stirring in
hope and thoughtfulness. Blend together with
forgiveness. Bake with hugs and kisses.
Serve daily in generous portions.

PEACH COBBLER (SHORTCUTS)

Prep time: 20
Cook time: 35
Serves 4–6
Difficulty: 1 **2** 3 4 5

YOU WILL NEED:

4 Pillsbury pie crust (thawed
    and rolled out)
1 casserole dish or aluminum
    pan (*not a cake pan*)
4 15.25 oz cans of Del Monte
    sliced peaches (2 cans
    drained completely)

¾ cup of dark brown sugar
½ cup of granulated sugar
3 tbsp of cinnamon
½ tbsp of nutmeg
1 egg
1 tbsp of water

- Preheat oven to 350.
- In a large pot, over medium-to-high heat, add peaches, sugar, cinnamon, and nutmeg.
- Heat to a simmer, stirring frequently.
- Line the bottom of the casserole dish with 2 pie crusts (pie crusts will overlap).
- Remove peaches from the stovetop and pour over the top of pie crusts.
- Whisk together the egg and water.
- Cover peaches with remaining pie crusts.
- Using a paring knife or fork, create a few vents in the crusts.
- Brush pie crusts with egg wash.
- Bake for 30-35 minutes or until cobbler is bubbling and golden brown.

PEACH PIE WITH PEACH CROWN ROYAL (21+ DESSERT)

Prep time: 20 minutes
Cook time: 35 minutes
Serves 2–4
Difficulty: 1 2 **3** 4 5

YOU WILL NEED:

1 Pillsbury pie crust (thawed and rolled out)
1 deep-dish pie shell
2 15.25 oz cans of Del Monte sliced peaches (drained completely)
½ cup of dark brown sugar
¼ cup of granulated sugar
1 tbsp of cinnamon
½ tbsp of nutmeg
2 oz of Peach Crown Royal
1 egg
1 tbsp of water

- Preheat oven to 350.
- In a large pot, over medium-to-high heat, add peaches, sugar, cinnamon, nutmeg, and Crown Royal.
- Heat to a simmer while stirring frequently.
- Remove peaches from the stovetop and pour them into the pie shell.
- Whisk together egg and water and then set aside.
- Using a pizza cutter or knife, cut pie crust into 1-inch strips.
- Alternate strips over peaches, creating a basket weave.
- Use a fork or the back of a spoon and pinch the edges of the pie together.
- Lightly brush the top of the strips and edges with the egg wash.
- Bake for 30–35 minutes or until golden brown.
- Remove from oven and allow to cool before serving.

APPLE PIE WITH APPLE CIROC (21+ DESSERT)

Prep time: 20 minutes
Cook time: 35 minutes
Serves
Difficulty: 1 2 **3** 4 5

YOU WILL NEED:

1 Pillsbury pie crust (thawed
   and rolled out)
1 deep-dish pie shell
2 15.25 oz cans of Del Monte sliced
   peaches (drained completely)
⅛ cup of brown sugar

⅛ cup of granulated sugar
½ tbsp of cinnamon
¼ tbsp of nutmeg
2 oz of Apple Ciroc
1 egg
1 tbsp of water

- Preheat oven to 350.
- In a large pot, over medium to high heat, add peaches, sugar, cinnamon, nutmeg, and Apple Ciroc.
- Heat to a simmer while stirring frequently.
- Remove peaches from the stovetop and pour them into the pie shell.
- Whisk together egg and water and then set aside.
- Cover apples with pie crust.
- Using a fork or knife, vent the center of the pie.
- Use a fork or the back of a spoon and pinch the edges of the pie together.
- Lightly brush the top and edges with egg wash.
- Bake for 30–35 minutes or until golden brown.
- Remove from oven and allow to cool before serving.

STRAWBERRY SHORTCAKE
(*SHORTCUTS)

Prep time: 10 minutes
Cook time: 10 minutes
Serves 2–4
Difficulty: **1** 2 3 4 5

YOU WILL NEED:

1-2 Entenmann's all-butter loaf cake
2 cans of strawberry pie filling
16 oz of Original Cool Whip
   (refrigerated, not frozen)

1 lb of fresh strawberries (cleaned)
1 loaf pan
Ghirardelli strawberry syrup
Vanilla ice cream (optional)

- Slice cake into ½ inch slices.
- Place cake slices in a single layer in the bottom of the loaf pan.
- Spread a layer of Cool Whip on top of the cake.
- Next, layer with strawberry pie filling.
- Repeat steps 2 through 4 until the loaf pan is almost filled, leaving approximately 1 inch from the top.
- On top of the final layer (which should be strawberries), spread one last layer of Cool Whip.
- Cover with plastic wrap and freeze for up to 30 minutes, just until firm *but not frozen!*
- Remove from freezer.
- Remove plastic wrap and decorate the top with fresh strawberries.
- Slice and plate.
- Add a scoop of vanilla ice cream.
- Drizzle with strawberry syrup and serve.

FUN, FAMILY, AND KID-FRIENDLY RECIPES

PEPPERONI FLATBREAD PIZZA

Prep time: 10 minutes
Cook time: 10–13 minutes
Serves 2–4
Difficulty: 1 **2** 3 4 5

YOU WILL NEED:

1 pk of artisan flatbread
24 oz of Bertolli marinara sauce
6 oz of sliced pepperoni
16-24 oz of Kraft creamy melt
   mozzarella cheese

Oregano
Crushed red pepper flakes (optional)
Extra virgin olive oil

- Preheat oven to 350–375.
- Place flatbread on pizza pan or baking tray.
- Using a large spoon or ladle, spread marinara sauce over flatbread.
- Sprinkle the desired amount of mozzarella cheese on top of the sauce, saving a little cheese for the top of pizza.
- Arrange the desired amount of pepperoni on top of the cheese.
- Sprinkle the remaining cheese on top.
- Sprinkle with oregano.
- Bake for 10–13 minutes or until cheese is melted.
- Remove from oven.
- Drizzle with extra virgin olive oil.
- Slice and serve.

CINNAMON ROLL DONUTS AND DONUT HOLES

Prep time: 10 minutes
Cook time: 5 minutes
Serves 2–4
Difficulty: 1 **2** 3 4 5

YOU WILL NEED:

Vegetable oil
1 can Pillsbury cinnamon rolls

1 round cookie cutter (small)
Powdered sugar

- Heat vegetable oil in a medium pot.
- Remove cinnamon rolls from the canister and place on a cutting board.
- Using a small, round cookie cutter, cut a hole in the center of the cinnamon rolls. *Do not discard the centers!*
- Once the oil is hot, carefully add 2–4 cinnamon rolls to the oil. *Do not overcrowd!*
- Fry until golden brown, approximately for 1–2 minutes per side.
- Remove from oil and transfer to a paper towel.
- Once slightly cooled, transfer to a plate.
- Heat cinnamon roll cream cheese icing for 10–15 seconds in the microwave. *Remove metal top before microwaving!*
- Remove icing from the microwave. *Do it with caution as contents may be hot!*
- Drizzle donuts with cinnamon roll icing (save remaining icing for donut holes) and sprinkle with powdered sugar.

FOR DONUT HOLES:

- Form the centers of the cinnamon rolls into balls.
- Add the cinnamon roll balls to oil.
- Fry until golden brown for about 1–2 minutes.
- Remove from oil and transfer to a paper towel.
- While still warm, roll donut holes in powdered sugar until completely covered.
- Use remailing icing for dipping.
- Serve and enjoy!

CLASSIC GRILLED CHEESE

Prep time: 5 minutes
Cook time: 5 minutes
Serves 2
Difficulty: **1** 2 3 4 5

YOU WILL NEED:

4 slices of your favorite bread
4 slices of Gouda cheese (divided)
4 slices of Cheddar cheese (divided)

2 tbsp of butter or spread (softened)
Parsley (for garnish)

- Butter 1 side of each slice of bread.
- On unbuttered side of bread, layer 2 slices of gouda and 2 slices of cheddar.
- Place second slice of bread on top, butter side facing up.
- Repeat steps for second sandwich
- In heated skillet, place sandwiches butter side down, cover (this helps cheese to melt), and heat until golden brown about 3-4 minutes
- Use a spatula and flip sandwich.
- Cover and heat until golden brown.
- Remove from heat and transfer to plate.
- Slice sandwiches diagonally.
- Sprinkle with parsley for garnish.
- Serve with tomato soup (optional).

NUTELLA, BANANA, AND JELLY SANDWICH

Prep time: 5 minutes
Cook time: 5 minutes
Serves 2
Difficulty: **1** 2 3 4 5

YOU WILL NEED:

4 thick slices of bread
Nutella chocolate hazelnut spread

1 medium to large banana
  (sliced and divided)
Strawberry jelly or jam

- Spread 2 slices of bread with Nutella chocolate hazelnut spread.
- Add banana slices to each slice of bread with Nutella spread.
- Spread the remaining 2 slices of bread with strawberry jelly or jam.
- Place bread with strawberry or jam on top of the Nutella and banana slices, making a sandwich.
- Slice each sandwich diagonally and plate.
- Serve with a glass of cold milk (optional).

CHOCOLATE CHIP COOKIE ICE CREAM SANDWICH

Prep time: 10 minutes
Cook time: 11–13 minutes
Makes 6–8
Difficulty: 1 **2** 3 4 5

YOU WILL NEED:

30 oz Nestle Toll House cookie dough
10 oz Nestle Toll House mini semi-sweet chocolate chip morsels
10.5 oz rainbow sprinkles

1 pint vanilla ice cream (or flavor of your choice), softened
Parchment paper
Ziplock freezer bags or freezer-safe container

- Preheat oven to 350.
- Line a cookie sheet with nonstick aluminum foil.
- Slice cookie dough into ½ inch slices. *Note: Slicing the cookie dough will give the cookies a close-to-perfect circle when baking.*
- Place cookie slices on the cookie sheet.
- Bake for 11–13 minutes
- While cookies are baking, in separate bowls, empty chocolate chip morsels and sprinkles.
- Remove cookies from oven and allow to cool completely.
- Once cooled, scoop the desired amount of ice cream on top of 3–4 cookies
- Place another cookie on top, thus creating an ice cream sandwich.
- Roll the sides of the ice cream sandwich in the bowl of chocolate chip morsels and/or sprinkles (you may need to do this 2–3 times).

- Place the ice cream sandwiches in a freezer bag or freezer-safe container, separating the ice cream sandwiches with parchment paper. This will prevent the sandwiches from sticking together.
- Freeze for at least 30–45 minutes.
- Remove from the freezer and enjoy!

MEET THE AUTHOR

I grew up in Southeast, Washington, DC. as an only child in a single-parent household. As an only child, I've always had a compassion to help others. Having such compassion led me to a career in law enforcement—a career that lasted thirty years! However, I had a much deeper and stronger connection with food. My desire to cook was out-of-this-world. Oddly enough, I never went to culinary school. I'd watch my grandmother prepare feasts for the family every Sunday like it was Thanksgiving. She'd teach me how to add just the right amount of seasonings, what temperature I should set in the oven, and even how long I should stir the sauce. This only enhanced my desire to cook. It was relaxing for me. The kitchen was my "happy place."

While I learned the basics from my grandmother, I did pick up a few helpful tips when I was in high school. I attended Theodore Roosevelt High School. Back then, the school had a career and trade program and one on travel and tourism–hotel and restaurant management. I studied this from tenth to twelfth grade. But after graduating, I went straight into the police cadet program. Now retired, I'm right back to what I enjoy most—cooking! Don't get me wrong. I've definitely enjoyed my career in law enforcement and being able to help others, but my heart has always been in the kitchen. I've always thought that food was comforting to the soul and that food brings people closer together. By sharing a few recipes, I can help do just that. Now let's be clear, if you are looking for a five-star cuisine and an eight-course meal, then you have stumbled upon the wrong cookbook 'cause I ain't got it, lol! Remember earlier when I said I never went to culinary school? Oh, OK. Just a friendly reminder.

Seriously, I want people to experience what I experienced with my grandmother: to be able to cook from the heart and the depths of your soul and enjoy it!

Printed in the United States
by Baker & Taylor Publisher Services